THE LITTLE OWL
& THE BIG TREE

A CHRISTMAS STORY

Jonah Winter • Jeanette Winter

Beach Lane Books

New York   London   Toronto   Sydney   New Delhi

There once was an owl who lived in a tree.

The owl didn't have a name—
and of course she didn't:
She was a wild animal.

Specifically, she was a Northern Saw-whet Owl,
the tiniest owl in the eastern United States.

She was so tiny, in fact,
it's doubtful anybody knew she existed.
She slept all day in a hole in the tree—

and hunted at night.

She was alone.
She was peaceful.

Then one day, everything changed.
She was woken from her slumber
by the sounds of voices and power tools.

Suddenly her tree began to move—
creaking and shaking.

Now the tree was falling down!

It was loaded onto a truck
and driven away—
with the owl inside her little hole,
inside the big bundled tree.

The noise of the truck on the highway
was unlike anything this owl had ever heard.
Hours went by,
with the rumbling and the noise and the motion.

At last the motion stopped.
The noise had changed—
strange and new:
honking horns, people shouting, music blaring.

The owl was still in her hole,
wondering what in the world was going on.

Once again, there were voices, up close,
and just like that,
the wrapping was being removed.

Finally, the owl came out of her hole—

only to find herself face to face with a *man*!

The two of them stared at each other for a while.
And when the man realized the owl was not flying away,

he reached over and held the owl in his hand.

And still, the owl didn't fly away.
She was tired and hungry—
she hadn't eaten in days.

The man found a box and placed the owl inside it,
along with some pine twigs.
And still, the owl didn't fly away.

And she didn't fly away
when she was taken in a car by the kind man's wife
to a wildlife rescue center.

At the wildlife center,
the owl looked up from her box
to see a woman looking down at her.

The woman fed her and gave her water—
and made sure she wasn't hurt.

The woman left her alone in a room
with some mice, the owl's favorite food.
She was a wild animal, after all,
and had to get used to feeding herself again.

Meanwhile, her old home, the tree,
was now the Christmas tree
in New York City's Rockefeller Center!
And she, the tiny owl, was famous.

She now had a name: Rockefeller.
She didn't know anything about that, though.
She knew about being an owl.
And when she'd regained her strength,

she was released near the wildlife rescue center.
It wasn't her old home—
but at least she was back in the wild,
back in the trees,

somewhere out there under the stars.

AUTHOR'S NOTE

On November 12, 2020, a seventy-five-foot-tall spruce tree was chopped down in the town of Oneonta in New York State. Inside this enormous tree there was a tiny adult Northern Saw-whet Owl. Saw-whet Owls often occupy small, cave-like spaces within the trunks of such trees. The tree and the owl were loaded onto a truck, which traveled 170 miles and arrived at Rockefeller Center in New York City on November 14. Once there, the tree remained on the truck until November 16, when the owl was discovered by Jason Ramos, a worker removing the tarp from the tree and preparing it to be decorated for Christmas. Having gone a few days without food or water, the owl was weak and in a state of shock, which is no doubt why she allowed herself to be handled by humans. She was taken to the Ravensbeard Wildlife Center, a couple of hours north of New York City, and was nurtured back to health for a week by Ellen Kalish, who then released this now-famous bird back into the wild on November 24.

In loving memory of
Edward Pennington Denmead,
who loved birds
—Jonah Winter

To Elisa Shokoff
—Jeanette Winter

BEACH LANE BOOKS

An imprint of Simon & Schuster Children's Publishing Division • 1230 Avenue of the Americas, New York, New York 10020 • Text © 2021 by Jonah Winter • Illustration © 2021 by Jeanette Winter • Book design © 2021 by Simon & Schuster, Inc. • All rights reserved, including the right of reproduction in whole or in part in any form. • BEACH LANE BOOKS and colophon are trademarks of Simon & Schuster, Inc. • For information about special discounts for bulk purchases, please contact Simon & Schuster Special Sales at 1-866-506-1949 or business@simonandschuster.com. • The Simon & Schuster Speakers Bureau can bring authors to your live event. For more information or to book an event, contact the Simon & Schuster Speakers Bureau at 1-866-248-3049 or visit our website at www.simonspeakers.com. • The text for this book was set in ClassicXtraRound-Bold. • Manufactured in China • 0721 SCP • First Edition • 10 9 8 7 6 5 4 3 2 1 • Library of Congress Control Number 2021009597 • ISBN 9781665902137 • ISBN 9781665902144 (ebook)